LIFE AS A *Mosaic*

POEMS OF ECSTASY, ELEGY AND EVERYTHING IN BETWEEN

Gia Porwal

ISBN 979-8-88805-492-5

This book is dedicated to my loved ones especially, my *Mom* & *Dad* for their endless efforts, affection, and constant encouragement. Thank you for teaching me to believe in myself, in God, and in my dreams.

To my *Dada-Dadi & Nana-Nani*,
for blessing me and loving me endlessly.

To my partner in crime, my love, my sister, *Viha*,
for placing my thoughts on sibling bond in words.

Special Credits to *Ms. Rachna Narang* for guiding me through the process of writing.

My heartfelt gratitude to *Ajal Al- Mareefah International School* (Jazan, KSA) and teachers for providing me the best eduction and making me what I am today.

Thanks to all my readers for believing in me
and reading my work.

Contents

I. Season Poems

Stingy Summer

Yay! It's summer, no school,
I can't wait to go to the pool.
But the bugs around sting bad,
Oh! All the mosquitoes make me mad!
They are like vampires in miniature things,
Why, why, why? Did God let them have wings?

And nobody forgot the enormous crowds,
Also, their rackets are very loud.
Who knows what illnesses they have,
Why, why, why? Can't clouds start to clave?

Sleep, as a matter of fact, extinct,
Like last night I barely blinked.
My eyes are bitter with this every night routine,
Why, why, why? Is the Sun so keen?

We sweat, we stink,
Now summer has reached its brink,
How can summer be so rude?
Why, why, why? I ask in a furious mood.

Scorching sun burns like furnaces,
All around, causing utter disturbance.
Bye! Bye! Summer is what I want to say,
Why, why, why? Can't summer just go away?

Spring Vibes

Hearing melodies of birds chirping,
Flapping their wings on a twig,
Admiring tree's new wig,
They are enjoying the cool breeze.

I saw a doe frolicking,
In the lush green meadow,
Bright Sun beaming with angelic glow,
How many surprises it will bring,
I don't know!

I felt the blushing petals brushing against,
Going on about their beauty,
Oh! How can they say thanks to nature?
For always fulfilling her duties.

I thought the Sun was hugging the wind,
With clouds floating above the blue sea,
I hear all the flower buds going *wee*,
All kids whispering to the breeze,
It's so peaceful it puts my mind at ease.

The Majestic Rain

How beautiful is the rain!
Giving respite from heat and pain.
The rain is the giving of heaven,
People while dancing in it feel awakened.

How pleasant is the majestic rainbow!
Always standing high, not low.
Most people drink hot chocolate,
Sitting on the balcony enjoying every droplet.

Cleaning everything around,
Such thunder of yours can scare a hound.
Giving a tint of light to the grey skies,
Lightning, it fries.

Rain is kind to land,
We will pray for you hand in hand.
Silver droplets give us life,
From heat and dust, it gives respite.

Welcome Winter

The cold crisp winter,
Breaks Fall into splinters.
It brings chills into the air.
Welcoming winter there.

All animals hide in holes,
Sleeping in paradise,
Waking up when winter rolls,
Resting till spring calls.

Sitting alongside a burning fire,
Watching the snowflakes dance.
The chilly wind blowing all around,
Making you want to go out at every chance.

Christmas fills the white canvas with colours,
Bringing out the joy of winter.
The snowflakes play, and the winds sway,
To make it the happiest night of the year.

II. Elements of Nature Poems

Wonderful Trees

Trees are the Earth's lungs,
Animals around them have fun,
It gives food to the needy,
And provides us with greenery.

On their branches, birds make their nest,
Under your warmth we all rest,
You have a brown thick trunk,
The water you provide to be drunk.

You provide us with colourful fruits,
Deep down are your thick roots,
We have fun running around you,
Your branches spread vastly in the sky blue.

Trees, you give us air to breathe,
Still, we cut you for our greed,
Work you do so much,
And surprisingly without any fuss.

Thank you trees for your care,
You are definitely so fair,
I will always protect you,
From the damage people do.

Fire

Burning and burning,
Its flames frolicking about.
Twisting and turning are its flow,
Oh my! How vivid is its glow?

Eyes lit by blazes of hope,
Murdering the shyness inside,
Seen by the adoption of one's mind,
It could be peaceful or unkind.

Fire god is always giving,
Its flames in the winds singing.
It is of course a good slave,
As a master quite damaging.

That fills with light,
Glistering and intense,
Everyone it can inspire,
So, beware, for it is fire.

Earth Day Everyday

Earth, the third planet closest to the Sun,
So fascinating and the only one.
Revolving, revolting for seasons and days,
Earth never fails, to amaze me.

It gives water, air and soil,
But we mix it with dirty oil.
We scheme our nature's death,
But the ultimate destruction could be our breath.

So, let's grow trees instead of factories,
Become a family instead of boundaries.
Let's save the Earth in different ways,
And make it Earth Day every day.

Sunshine

Another perfect day,
To let the sunshine pass.
Through my body to make it feel like clay,
Calm, soothing.

I let its warm ray touch my skin,
Freeing me from the cold.
Talking me out of dark fins,
Dreamy relaxing.

Its yellow colour,
Soothes me in life.
Away from what is duller,
Resting, feeling.

Smooth tingling light,
Untangling, tangled emotions.
The path is always right,
Trust, truth.

III. Festive Poems

Merry Christmas

A shining star flew down,
Merrily spreading news around.
The "Son of GOD" is born,
Whose news adorned us all.

The saviour of Earth is here,
To him every person is dear.
Peace and happiness, he showers,
That secures us in our happy hours.

Red and white candy cones,
Let's celebrate in our joyful zones.
Looking for the light of Rudolf's nose,
Has anybody ever seen it? Who knows!

Without Santa Christmas is all wrong,
Why did he come so late? I long.
All families singing carols,
Sitting together learning morals.

Children playing with toys all night,
Or even picking up on pillow fights.
Cakes and cookies are served,
Sweet treats everyone deserves.

The decorated trees like bright sky,
Under which Santa's carriage flies,
Spreading joy that makes us believe,
To embrace all of Christmas eve!

Holi Hai!

The advent of spring brings joy,
Holi is here for us to enjoy,
Splish-splash, splish-splash,
Let's have a hearty bash!

Festivals of colours, balloons, and buckets,
Relishing the treats of *Gujiyas*, cutlets,
Coloured water fills the water guns,
Let the harmful colours be shunned.

Ketchup for Red, henna for green,
Make your celebration worth seeing.

Sprinklers drench us thru and thru,
Oh God! I might get down with the flu,
Let this Holi be eco-friendly,
And treat Nature gently.

IV. Limerick Poems

Stubborn Rose

There was once a rose,
Who stood in a stylish pose,
Until she got plucked,
She thought she never sucked.
And wriggled in front of the nose.

Rude Sun

Why is the sky in a melancholy mood?
Did it fight with the Sun, who is so often rude?
Sun frowns at the wind and clouds,
Moon finds him unpleasantly loud,
Stars too think he is crude.

Kate

A woman called Kate,
Could not find a roommate.
She searched for hours,
Under the ocean and on top of towers.
What can she do with her fate?

V. Story Poems

The Giant Beast

Once there was a giant beast,
Who lived merrily in the South-east,
He used to gobble up people,
And stole things from a steeple.

Communities were scared of him,
Calling naughty children by his name Tim,
He used to get thrilled by that,
Celebrate by dancing on rats.

One day came a woman kind and bold,
She killed Tim, everyone told.
With the giant's head, she came,
In town, she got fame.

Elders were amazed by this,
Asking, "How did you do it, Miss?"
"With help of Rose - The Giant, I did it,"
She was very strong and fit.

How did she make friends with a giant?
Oh! She answered, "Rose is my massage client."
Children took her as an inspiration,
She took this to a real aspiration.

Flying merrily in the town,
Spreading joy to ones in frown.
Now this story got to an end,
Bye-bye, salute all my friends.

Lion's Ministry

Mighty Lion was the forest's king,
Every forest animal was his subject,
Showering him with gifts and rings,
His strength brought tremendous effects.

Majestic king approached the fox,
Wanted him to lead as Home Minister.
Exclaimed loud, "fox think outside the box,"
You are clever, cunning with siniters.

He summoned next to the panther,
You are strong and agile.
Defense minister is given to you,
As your strength is true.

The next in the minister row,
Was the flying and mighty-eyed crow.
Foreign minister was given to him,
Crow then said not to be grim.

The three ministers together swore,
They will protect forests more and more.
The king to promised them,
To keep them safe in his realm,

Men from Scion

There was a man from Scion 4,
He wanted to visit all shores,
But he had a concert everyday live,
So, he went to Scion 5.

His friend from Scion 5,
To travel he thrived,
So, he ventured to Scion 6,
But there he was stuck in a fix.

The friend's friend in Scion 6,
Wanted to show off marvellous tricks,
Soon he flew up to Scion 7,
He knew his name rhymed, Kevin.

Kevin's friend in Scion 7,
Swam fast to Scion 11,
Kept travelling to different Scions,
Ended up living in Lyon.

Monster

Dares, dares, dares,
Is all that the golden generation cares.
Sarah happened to be a victim,
Of this violence.

How she thinks of stepping into my castle,
A filthy girl competing with a vassal.
How can she believe she will get out,
She better fill with doubt.

I pull her within with all force,
What should I do with her?
She is a course,
I made her future blur.

I whisper it is okay,
To bring fear.
When she closes her eyes,
Her memories I tear.

Slowly, softly she closes her eyes,
Rocking back and forth.
I let my power rise,
And break her mind.

I push her out,
Command her to shout,
I hear the sirens,
Here to help a helpless girl.

She peers out of the window,
You can see me in books.
But not her,
She notices my smiles and deadly looks.

Horror Poem

So, I entered the scary expansion,
The continuation of a bone-chilling mansion.
To uncover the truth left behind,
What exists and what will I find?

A blood-curdling chuckle welcomes my way,
Oh! Look how these ugly faces sway.
Drip-drop, Drip-drop, the blood's sound,
What will be here? What will be found?

Spiders on cobwebs all about,
This no doubt is haunted.
Bodies here, bodies there,
Today, life I think is incredibly unfair.

Step by step quiet as a mouse,
Searching in this haunted house,
The mansion has its own mind,
What all exists and what will I unwind?

VI. Diamante Poems

Mother

Helpful, Funny,
Loving, Listening, Helping,
Chef, Friend, Fun, Sports,
Laughing, Pranking, Partying,
Naughty, Intelligent,
Child.

Writer

Imaginative, Prolific,
Creating, Scribbling, Editing,
Manuscript, Keyboard, Character, Genres,
Reading, Teaching, Engaging,
Interesting, Boring,
Book.

Plant

Tall, peaceful,
Growing, reaping, giving,
Fruit, producer, companion, ferocious,
Frolicking, howling, helping,
Friendly.

Moon

Misty, cool.
Glowing, haunting, changing.
Orbiter, creator, happier, shiner,
Vibing, giving, heating.
Bright, beautiful,
Sun.

VII. Dystopian Poems

In a World Full of Chaos

It drains the laughter,
It drains all the fun.
It hypnotizes everyone,
Chaos is here …

Violence - the normal calm,
Fight the new balm.
A crown on the world,
Chaos is here …

No comforting hugs,
No word such as love.
Nothing fun everything behooves,
Chaos is here …

Craving for freedom is restricted,
Nothing happy, as the council predicted.
Our world is filled with fear,
Why can't freedom be here?

Darkness is Rising

Darkness is rising,
Rising from under the Earth.
A new rebellion giving birth,
Darkness is rising.

The draught of dread,
Removed with no mercy.
Peace no longer has any courtesy,
Darkness is rising.

Fear is killing hope,
Violence is killing love.
The peace sign is no longer a dove,
Darkness is rising.

The doomed world,
Trapped in the dark cell.
This is the day our happiness fell,
'Cause darkness is rising.

VIII. Cinquain Poems

Book

Interesting, Catchy,
Reading, Writing, Editing,
Filled with imagination,
Writer.

Superwomen

Strong, Supportive,
Cooking, Caring, Helping,
Backbone of every house,
Mom.

Language

Pillar, Strength,
Learning, Reading, Trying,
Pride of every citizen,
Teacher.

Candle

Bright, Shine,
Uplifting, Pacifying, Purifying,
Enlightens every corner,
Flame.

IX. Child's Perception Poems

Cloud, My friend

Look! The little friends in the skies,
I can't get them despite all my tries,
It's a mystery how far they are!
Or are they the dress of the stars?

Look! They can't stand in one place,
My teacher would shout if they were my classmates.
I want to climb on their backs,
Chatting, gossiping and eating snacks.

I want to be its bosom friend,
Things of ours to each other we will lend
My father will bring one cloud for me,
And together we will sit and play Tea!

What-if ...

What-if the Earth flew off its orbit,
Would its atmosphere break down?
What-if a satellite would deorbit,
Would its country start to frown?

What-if humans had eight tentacles as legs,
Would we grow them back if they broke?
What-if we met someone and got them pegged,
Would we be friends the first time we met?

What-if dinosaurs came back to life,
Would all humans strive to live?
What-if we always start to strife,
Would all species ever learn to give?

What-if this?
What-if that?
All these questions strike us like a belief,
Who knows there might be more what-ifs ...

Whispering Sea

Is there a swimming pool here?
If not, what is it?
It seems so calm like nothing is to fear,
I wish we were so peaceful.

The waves crash with rocks,
Sprinkling water on us.
Sometimes it seems like it talks,
Whispering its secrets.

It eats the Sun every evening,
I guess it always stays hungry.
I wonder what's wrong with the moon,
Would the sea eat it soon?

How do the fishes breathe?
In the water so deep.
Oh! It's so calm,
Better than a lullaby to sleep.

X. Family Love Poems

Ode to Mother

You held my hand to walk me through,
To see the world completely true.
The fates I thank for having you,
Oh mother, see how much I grew!

You are always by my side,
Shaping my personality inside out.
The best prize I got was not a medal,
It was you - Mom, my life cycle's pedal.

An angel was sent to Earth,
How grateful I am for her birth!
The compassion she shows me every day,
Mother! Oh, how can I repay?

You sow a seed of self-control,
Every time you have to say no,
The values you plant nourish my soul.
You teach me all you know.

My dreams you share,
How obliged I am for your care.
Mom is such a unique word,
The most comforting in the world.

Ode to Father

A dad is someone who,
No matter how old you are.
Will catch you when you fall,
Any time at any call.

Dad, you helped me grow,
But we have a long way yet to go.
You are the one that makes sure we're okay,
And are always keen to lead the world.

You joke around,
And brighten my day,
The power you have to extinguish my frown
You turn blue my skies that are grey.

All the time you've been there,
You never fail to show your care.
I am obliged for what you do,
I am blessed to have a father like you.

Sibling Love

Don't think of pranking your sis,
'Cause your life will run out of bliss,
Don't think of stashing her clothes,
Otherwise, you will go where chaos goes.

Don't eat her favourite food,
Or you prove yourself as crude.
Don't hide her favourite books,
Or you'll lose your looks.

Together partners in crime,
No matter where in time,
Bullies to each other,
That's how it is with a sister or brother.

Don't irritate your sister,
And fill her with blisters.
So, whatever you do,
Or she'll do something worse to you.

Ode to Family

A family is so special,
In every possible way.
It's full of close friends,
I cherish them every day.

A family is made by heart,
Not by birth certificates or slips.
Family is the symbol of togetherness,
They walk through hard and happy trips.

Every family is different,
Like a stick-together kind.
They help each other,
In every way they find.

So, no matter what comes,
Arguments, laughter or knives.
You can always rely on one thing,
Family is for life.

Friendship

Something, not a laser could cut,
Helps you erase all your buts.
Something a cat cannot scratch,
Too strong for anyone to detach.

A feeling as pure as an angel,
A bond too bold to split.
All time this is faithful,
Everyone admires it.

It's like a tree, a saw can't bring down.
When someone is poor,
It is their crown.
Choose it carefully or it might leave you sour.

The light to your darkness,
A pleasant or painful trip.
It never leaves you with unusual starkness,
Oh god! Please give everyone friendship.

Memorable Road Trips

We pack our bags,
And stuff them in,
Our car's little trunk.
Stuffing them as we grin.

We sit with glee,
And pull out our music collection.
Listening, singing with affection,
It's time we all are free.

Like a true family,
We sit and learn.
About the world around us,
And look out during turns.

All snacks allowed,
To the sweetness of chocolate.
To the crunchiness of chips,
Seeing them makes my stomach flip.

The hotel is on the GPS maps,
I guess this is the end.
But oh, this place is monotonous,
Who can we play with if not our friends?

XI. School Poems

Ode to Books

To be enchanted in your engaging play,
Is the dream, I recover from every day.
Music, dances, spells and magic,
Occupy vast space in my head.
Making it so spacious for you,
Is something I will never dread.

Each night, I sleep,
With a plot twist in my mind.
You are the best lullaby,
Anyone can find.
Reading is the world to me,
In my imagination, it is the biggest key.

The night seems long.
But with you, my friend,
Nothing ever seems wrong.
With all this, I can say no more,
But I will ask you, readers:
Which book do you adore?

Exams!

Fiddling around with a pen in my hand,
Looking at my revision sheet for errands,
Searching my brain for all the answers,
Pinching myself when I find advancers.

Not able to leave studies and have fun,
I hate that time in tons.
No friends, no television is just a start,
Of trying to make us crazy smart.

The person who invented the exam was insane,
Sometimes I wonder if he had a brain.
He did this to make kids go lunatic,
Or it might be a backfired trick.

Exams! Exams! When the hell will they expire?
Otherwise, my head will get fire.
They will turn our brains into scrambled eggs,
And slowly start making a mind with threads.

With all this chaos and fuss,
Exams are important for all of us!

Listen Mr. Bully!

This is a no-bully zone,
If you're a bully, read this one.
Being cool doesn't mean expensive phones,
It is peace that we should weave.

Words too hurt really bad,
We want to help you,
So, tell us why you're sad,
We can heal the madness that grew.

I hope you see the good inside,
Deep down I see in you,
Through all the selfishness and pride.
I hope you see it too.

You punch and throw us to the ground,
This is a cruel thing.
You are nailing, a hobby newly found,
But you aren't the school king.

So, listen Mr. Bully stop,
Being insensitive, have fun,
Take care of this mess,
So, we can be friends.

Teamwork

Teamwork is our friendship,
All fun is experienced there.
How close it brings will make you flip.
Making you realize, how much you care.

A team is created,
With different personalities.
Sometimes it's not what anyone stated,
But everyone turns into buddies.

The work is filled with jokes,
Or occasional fights,
With every time you folks!
Or speaking about their rights.

Spending restless days working,
Brainstorming ideas really fast.
It's hard to think when your mind is lurking,
'Cause peace and rest are in the past.

All hopes up for the teacher to see,
Getting an A is a dream.
Making a silent plea,
These are the wonders of a team.

XII. Miscellaneous Poems

Glorious Egypt

A place I admire,
Everyone can inspire.
"I will definitely go," I say,
To the land of grand Pyramids.
A place where mighty river flows,
Where paper was by leaves made,
A community where *Amun Ra* was prayed.

"One must go and wander," I say,
Where it is torrid in May.
In ancient times when people died,
Rich and respected were mummified.
They were sent to the land of the dead,
In ceremonies, parchments were read.

Visiting a place of history,
Wow! It's full of mystery.
Egyptians are blessed with the river Nile,
Their lands are so very fertile,
Thinking of the past makes them smile.

Tour a place with picturesque tombs,
Thank you so writers of Rosetta stone,
How to read hieroglyphics is now world-known.

Ode to Women

To have wit as strong as an ox,
We aren't born to be shut in a box.
After all, we are women who sing.
Women should be empowered!

We are as fearless as a lion.
An idol to all our scions.
Women represent a tree.
Giving warmth and care for free.

Being a woman is a real pride,
Don't be bothered about the thinking of the crowd.
To enjoy what we love is always allowed.
So, let's shout out loud.
Empowered and strong women,
Make the world an outstanding place.

Almighty

Known for his wisdom and Fame,
The Almighty is blessed with many names.
People pray to Him on daily basis,
As He can bless with whatever they praise.

He and his *Sakhas* were butter thieves,
Who loves to play mischief!
With peacock's feather on his head,
His stories are still read.

Mesmerizing *Brajwasi*'s with his flute music,
Along with *Radhe* he dances at *poornima* mosaic.
His reincarnation on earth has been boons,
By killing demons, proven truth always wins.

He the creator of all,
The Almighty God.
I bow my head in front of the lord,
Praying peace for one and all.

Life During Pandemic

How much I miss going out!
While taking photos with friends we used to pout.
In school, malls and parks,
We shared scary stories in the dark.

Our life was full of roller coasters,
Trying to complete things on our rosters.
Having family gatherings together,
Celebrating events even in bad weather.

An experiment went wrong at night,
Because of that our lives are tight.
Now we contact friends on zoom,
Being sad we're not in the same room.

This is enough for all the people,
Why can't they go to a temple?
I can't resist anymore,
2020's dreams are shattered and torn.
Hope has started building like a cup,
The scientists for the vaccine aren't giving up.

Essence of Freedom

I am a lark,
Flying around in the park,
If a cage comes my way,
It is not where I would stay.

I am blissful like a sun ray,
Melodically singing in the month of May.
If clouds come in my lane,
I bless the Earth with mighty rain.

Liberty for me was a lie,
I understand now how I love to fly.
Empathetic towards my friends in a cage,
My heart bleeds with sorrow and rage.

Caged birds sing for free rein,
As they are in deep pain.
I pray to the Almighty for their freedom,
As I don't want them to be glum.

Freedom is the sweet smell of a rose,
Spreading solace wherever it goes.
Human pals are now confined in their domes,
Have understood how important it is to roam.

While flying high in a cold breeze,
I wish peace for all species.
Rage and Anger we all don't need,
Freedom to spread wings is all we need.

Life As It Is

Yellow, green, grey and black,
Life is never on track.
Giving excitement and anxiety,
Providing us an extraordinary society.

Blue with a dejected sigh,
Yellow encourages to go high.
Red with a furious yell,
Green of a doing well.

How bright is the flame of hope,
distinguished in the inky hours?
With a bit of hope, we all will cope,
Life - you are all ours.

Let's kill the wrong inside,
Life is a rollercoaster ride.
Life is a befogging quiz,
But I love life as it is.

Life can be a bit ferny,
Wishing us miracles.
Life is an intellectual whiz,
But I love life as it is.

Taste of honey,
Taste of olives,
Life isn't funny,
But I love life as it is.

Ups and downs, turns and twists,
Life is full of mists.
And it freezes,
But I love life as it is.

Life is a box of chocolate,
With blessings and fates.
Life is milk with fizz,
But I love life as it is.

We all quit in dark places,
But a tiny grin can leave traces.
Life is harder than photosynthesis.
But I love life as it is.

Celebrating life is what we should do,
And not double-think this through.
For, life only comes once.
But I love life as it is.

3 Wishes

3 wishes just for me,
Granted for sure,
Makes me wonder what I care,
And what is don't?.

First, got me thinking,
For poverty to end.
And for the prejudices to mend,
Of the poor or the rich.

Second, I think for,
The loss of pollution.
And the world to be nourished green,
To undo what humans did before.

Lastly, I want to explore,
Me and the world.
To know myself to the core,
And to live life freely.